SCENIC NEW ZEALAND

SCENIC NEW ZEALAND

PHOTOGRAPHY BY ROB SUISTED

TEXT BY KATHY OMBLER

KOWHAI

First published in 2002 by New Holland Kowhai
an imprint of New Holland Publishers (NZ) Ltd
Auckland • Sydney • London • Cape Town

www.newhollandpublishers.com

218 Lake Road, Northcote, Auckland, New Zealand
14 Aquatic Drive, Frenchs Forest, NSW 2086, Australia
86 Edgware Road, London W2 2EA, United Kingdom
80 McKenzie Street, Cape Town 8001, South Africa

ISBN: 1 877246 92 1

Publishing manager: Renée Lang
Design: Dexter Fry
Editor: Pat Field

Colour reproduction by Colourscan (Singapore)
Printed by Tien Wah Press (Pte) Ltd

ENDPAPERS **Shingle beach, Miranda, Firth of Thames**
These sheltered shores are a refuge for birdlife.

PAGE 1 **Lake Brunner and Hohonu Range, Westland**
Kahikatea thrive in wet conditions surrounding
wetlands and lakes.

PAGES 2/3 **Marlborough Sounds**
Hidden waterways, or drowned river valleys, dissect
the hills of northernmost South Island.

PAGES 4/5 **Beech forest, Boundary Stream Scenic
Reserve, Hawke's Bay**
Lichen-laden red beech trees are characteristic of
many New Zealand forests.

PAGES 8/9 **Lake Wakatipu**
Looking into the Rees and Dart valleys. One of the
snow- and ice-fed southern lakes.

CONTENTS

SOUTH ISLAND

TASMAN

SEA

PACIFIC OCEAN

Farewell Spit

Golden Bay

ABEL TASMAN
NATIONAL PARK

KAHURANGI
NATIONAL PARK

Marlborough
Sounds

• Picton

Nelson •

Blenheim •

NELSON/
MARLBOROUGH

Lake
Rotoiti

Westport •

Lake
Rotoroa

NELSON LAKES
NATIONAL PARK

Cook Strait

Kaikoura Ranges

PAPAROA
NATIONAL PARK

Punakaiki •

WEST COAST

)(Lewis Pass

• Kaikoura

Greymouth •

Hokitika •

Lake
Brunner

)(Arthur's Pass

ARTHURS PASS
NATIONAL PARK

Okarito Lagoon

WESTLAND/TAI POUTINI
NATIONAL PARK

Fox Glacier •

• Franz Josef Glacier

CANTERBURY

• CHRISTCHURCH

AORAKI/MT COOK
NATIONAL PARK

▲ Aoraki/Mt Cook

Akaroa •

Banks
Peninsula

MT ASPIRING
NATIONAL PARK

Haast Pass)(

• Timaru

Milford Sound/
Piopiotahi •

Lake
Wanaka

Lake
Hawea

• Wanaka

• Oamaru

Queenstown •

Lake
Wakatipu

OTAGO

• Moeraki

FIORDLAND
NATIONAL PARK

SOUTHLAND

DUNEDIN •

Otago
Peninsula

CATLINS
FOREST PARK

Nugget Point

INVERCARGILL •

Foveaux Strait

RAKIURA
NATIONAL PARK

STEWART ISLAND/
RAKIURA

NEW ZEALAND

INTRODUCTION

New Zealanders are fortunate. Theirs is such a stunning location down in the Antipodes – a setting that continues to be a major drawcard for international visitors who return to it again and again.

Almost any form of travel through the country will provide a range of incomparable vistas. An inter-city road trip, for example, might entail driving through a sprawling desert of tussock and rock, with snow-covered volcanoes looming on the skyline. Or it might involve negotiating a coastal-hugging highway, where waves crash and fur seals cavort on rocks between the road and sea. One thing is certain: mountains, forests, lakes and rivers will inevitably feature in any New Zealand journey of significant length. And in between the peaks rolling green farmland, orchards and vine-yards complete the countryside mosaic.

Small, sparsely populated and extending from sub-tropical to subantarctic climes, New Zealand is crammed with diverse and dramatic natural land-scapes. From alpine wilderness and glaciers to the rainforests and beaches of the northern climes, and from volcanoes and geothermal fields to fiords and wetlands, New Zealand is a treasure trove of environ-mental niches and diverse scenic splendour.

Geophysically, New Zealand is a young country. Its mountains and forests remained isolated for centuries, left to the artistry of nature's touch, while other countries were being developed by human hand. Because of its remote location in the South Pacific the country's flora and fauna have evolved in isolation from the rest of the world. Only in the past few hundred years has the wild New Zealand landscape been explored by humans, both Polynesian and European, and even now much of it remains just that – wild.

This young and untamed state has engendered a special spirit among the people of the land (known as Kiwis after one of their unique flightless birds) who have traditionally exhibited a strong desire to protect the natural values they hold dear. From early times the ethic of conservation has been strong. Although young in terms of human settlement, New Zealand was one of the first countries in the world to embrace the concept of conservation, and has established an impressive network of national and forest parks, reserves, marine reserves and wildlife sanctuaries that protect the natural landscape and wildlife.

The three volcanic mountains of Tongariro form the nucleus of New Zealand's first and the world's fourth

national park, established over 100 years ago when Maori chief Te Heuheu Tukino IV (Horonuku) gifted the three sacred peaks to the Crown, to preserve them in perpetuity. Years later, Tongariro became the first in the world to be granted dual world heritage status for its natural and cultural values.

The international significance of New Zealand's natural heritage is recognised by the designation of several World Heritage Sites. These include Tongariro National Park, Te Wahi Pounamu (a massive southern region encompassing four national parks), and the chilly but unique wonders of the Subantarctic Islands.

The wildlife in this young and isolated land is special; over half the world's whale species migrate through New Zealand waters. Several species of dolphin including Hector's, the world's rarest dolphin, live around the country's lengthy coastline, and penguins and albatross nest in southern breeding grounds. Small islands provide sanctuaries for rare and special native species, such as the world's largest and rarest parrot, the kakapo. Then there are the birds that fill the forests, mountain regions, wetlands and estuaries, making the country a birdwatchers' delight.

Today, over one-third of New Zealand is legally protected as conservation land. Much of the rest of the country is a medley of rural landscapes. Rolling green dairy farm pastures and cropping land contrast with steep hill country sheep and cattle stations. Fertile plains throughout the country are filled with produce: orchards, herb farms, vegetable crops and vineyards.

New Zealanders happily contrive to share the magnificence and special features of their country. From small beginnings not so very long ago they have developed what is today a comprehensive and sophisticated tourism industry. Nature tourism, guided walks, whale and dolphin watch cruises, bird watching tours, cultural shows, farm stays, and home stays are just some of the choices, along with some more extreme adventure options. Take bungy jumping, white water rafting, black water rafting, 'dam dropping' or paragliding off mountains – whether it's underground, in the air or inside a volcano crater, there is no end to the Kiwi ingenuity that dreams up ever more extreme ways to thrill in the spectacular natural settings of the land. Complementing visitor experiences in New Zealand's natural environment is a hospitality industry that has moved ahead in leaps and bounds in recent years. Immigrants from Europe, Asia and the Pacific Islands have added their cosmopolitan flavours to local cuisine and culture. New Zealand wines are fêted internationally, and Kiwis chefs work with the finest fresh, local produce in restaurants and hotels throughout the country. With this abundance of experiences on offer to visitors, New Zealand is indeed the ultimate destination.

NORTH ISLAND

Although by far the most heavily populated island of New Zealand, the North Island contains a remarkable range of natural features. It is, it would be fair to say, an island of many contrasts. Over one million people, one-third of New Zealand's population, live in Auckland city. Yet just a few hours' drive south of city haze and motorways finds the lakes and geysers of geothermal Rotorua, then the vast, forested hinterland of Te Urewera. In the subtropical north rainforests are dominated by giant kauri trees, and beaches, inlets and islands dot the coastline.

In the centre of the island the Tongariro volcanoes stand like sentinels over surrounding forests and farms. These mountains are sacred to the Maori people, the foundation of New Zealand's national park system and the first World Heritage Area in the world to recognise both natural and cultural values. Further south, extending towards capital city and cosmopolitan Wellington, are tussock-covered mountain ranges. Throughout the island, scattered between its four national and 13 forest parks, are smaller cities, towns and regions of intensive farming, exotic forestry and horticulture.

PREVIOUS PAGES Mt Taranaki, Egmont National Park
The near-symmetrical volcano, Taranaki, towers like a
lonesome sentinel and dominates the landscape of
Taranaki province. Below the snowline, the mountain
is mantled with subalpine shrublands and, still lower,
towering popdocarp forests which feature New
Zealand's tallest tree, the kahikatea, or white pine.

**ABOVE Te Werahi Beach, Cape Maria van Diemen
and Motuopao Island, Far North**
Summer-flowering flax stands tall among the ground-
hugging native shrubs that cling to the ever-shifting
sand dunes of this windswept coast. This remote
coastline is one of New Zealand's most significant
wildlife habitats. Motuopao Island (far right) has been
declared a nature reserve to protect its breeding
colonies of prions and petrels.
A coastal walkway from Cape Reinga leads across Te
Werahi Beach, past Cape Maria van Diemen then turns
south towards Ninety Mile Beach.

RIGHT Cape Reinga, Far North
For over 60 years the Cape Reinga lighthouse has
shone its vital message to ships rounding this wild
and unpredictable northern tip of New Zealand, where
the Tasman Sea and Pacific Ocean come together in a
turbulent clashing of currents.
The cape itself, Te Rerengawairua, is of great spiritual
significance for it is from here, after death, that all
Maori spirits descend into the underworld (reinga) to
return to the land of their ancestors.

ABOVE **Ninety Mile Beach**
The sweep of camel-coloured sand actually extends an uninterrupted 102 kilometres. Behind the beach are great dunes whipped to a height of 100 metres and pushed a kilometre inland by prevailing westerly winds. This walker is fortunate to have solitude. Each day a host of tourist coaches drive along the beach en route to Cape Reinga.

LEFT **Mangonui Harbour, Doubtless Bay**
Pleasure craft and fishing boats shelter in historic Mangonui Harbour. In earlier days whaling ships called here for provisions, at a time when Maori lived in fishing settlements and fortified villages around the harbour. Mangonui is one of many sheltered anchorages along Northland's east coast. The small town here has a reputation for good cafés and fish and chip shops. It is a popular holiday town, although the permanent population is steadily growing as people discover the region's qualities.

ABOVE TOP **Cable Bay**
Except for summer holidays, the beaches of the Far
North are largely deserted but for the dolphins that
swim close to shore, and seabirds which nest and fish
in the bays. Cable Bay is so named because the first
New Zealand/Australia telephone cable was landed
here in 1902.

ABOVE BOTTOM **Sailing regatta, Taipa, Doubtless Bay**
New Zealand has a legacy of international yachting
success, be it in Olympic regattas, round the world
racing, Americas Cup or any other cup. Many of our
world-class sailors started small, racing tiny craft such
as this fleet, in bays and harbours around the country.

ABOVE Whare Runanga on Waitangi National Reserve

Whare Runanga is a 'meeting house' for all people. Carvings on the maihi (barge poles) and woven panels inside represent all the main Maori tribes. The Whare Runanga stands near where, in 1840, the Treaty of Waitangi was signed by British representatives and local Maori chiefs. The treaty, defining the partnership between Maori and the British Crown, was later signed by many other tribal chiefs. Over the years treaty-related issues have become contentious, and a governmental Waitangi Tribunal is now fully engaged hearing treaty grievances.

RIGHT TOP Waitangi National Reserve

Also known as the 'Birthplace of the Nation', Waitangi National Reserve occupies a commanding site over-looking the inner Bay of Islands. In the magnificent grounds visitors can explore the historic Treaty House (right), a large waka taua (war canoe) and the Whare Runanga, built in 1940 to commemorate the centennial of the signing of the Treaty of Waitangi.

RIGHT BOTTOM Motuarohia (Roberton Island)

Islands in the bay support a wealth of natural marine habitats. An 'underwater trail' designed specifically for snorkelling and the first of its kind in New Zealand is located in a sheltered lagoon on this tiny island.

FOLLOWING PAGES

LEFT Bottlenose dolphins, Bay of Islands

Hundreds of bottlenose, among the largest dolphin species in the world, live in the Bay of Islands.

RIGHT Tane Mahuta, Waipoua, Northland

Tane Mahuta, the world's largest kauri tree, is about 1500 years old, stands 51 metres tall and has a girth of over 13 metres.

ABOVE Sky Tower view
The 328 metre view. Auckland's Sky Tower, completed
in 1997, is the tallest structure in the southern hemisphere. A 40-second lift ride carries visitors up the
tower to a revolving restaurant and observation deck
to enjoy stunning 360 degree views of the city and the
Hauraki Gulf. (The glass floor panels are 44mm thick
and as strong as concrete.) At the tower's base there
are more restaurants and bars, a casino, theatre,
conference centre and hotel.

RIGHT Auckland city and Westhaven Marina
Corporate Auckland overlooks the city's largest boat
marina, with yachts poised for weekend explorations.
Auckland, New Zealand's largest city, has the highest
ratio of boat ownership of any city in the world, which
is understandable given the city's proximity to the
Hauraki Gulf, a magnificent expanse of sheltered
waterways and islands. The focus of recreational
boating and competitive sailing, the gulf is also
home to several flourishing and world-renowned
island wildlife sanctuaries.

LEFT **Auckland Harbour Bridge, Auckland**
Since 1959, the harbour bridge has linked Auckland
city with its North Shore suburbs. Traffic volumes
quickly exceeded expectation and four lanes were
added in 1969. As Auckland continues to grow the
possibility of building a second harbour bridge is a
regular topic of discussion.

ABOVE **Viaduct Basin, Auckland**
Near the heart of downtown Auckland, this sheltered
basin received a major overhaul when Team New
Zealand won the America's Cup. The basin has since
been a busy base for challenging cup crews and for
visiting yachts and luxury launches. The waterfront
surrounds, lined with cafés, bars and restaurants, is
a popular meeting place for locals and visitors alike.

ABOVE AND RIGHT **Whatipu Beach and Manukau Harbour entrance, west Auckland**
Surging seas, surf and sand bars combine to create a dangerous passage into the shelter of Manukau Harbour. For a brief time ships called to a wharf on Paratutae Island (top) to collect kauri timber from the ranges behind. Today, staunch surfers, beachcombers and wading birds are often the only signs of life. The green and gold coloured native pingao (right) is a sand-stabilising plant prized for weaving.

LEFT Waiheke Island
The enigma that is Auckland – it is the country's
largest urban metropolis yet islands such as Waiheke
are just a 40-minute ferry ride from downtown.
Waiheke is the most populated of the Hauraki Gulf
islands; city workers and weekend holidaymakers
commute by ferry to enjoy the beaches, wineries,
forest reserves and delightful outlooks over the gulf –
this view looks eastwards to the Coromandel
Peninsula.

ABOVE New Zealand Pigeon (kereru)
Known in Northland as kupapa, the native pigeon is
widespread throughout New Zealand, although in
some areas numbers have declined. The kereru is one
of the largest native birds, and the only one capable of
swallowing large fruits and seeds. It therefore plays
an important role in the seed dispersal of many large-
fruiting native trees, such as puriri, karaka and tawa
all of which play a part in ongoing re-afforestation
schemes on the Coromandel Peninsula and certain
islands in the gulf.

LEFT TOP **Cathedral Cove, Hahei**
The natural rock arch guards the entrance to a special
swimming spot; Cathedral Cove. Beyond the beach is
Te Whanganui a Hei (Cathedral Cove) Marine Reserve,
where several kilometres of reefs, underwater caves,
deep-water corals and a great diversity of marine life
are protected. To date there are 13 marine reserves in
New Zealand.

LEFT BOTTOM **Coromandel coast, near Thames**
Summertime around the northern New Zealand coast
is characterised by splashes of colour from the native
pohutukawa tree, also known as the New Zealand
Christmas tree.

ABOVE **Hahei Beach**
Earthworks from an old Maori site overlook swimmers
and boaties. Not far from this popular beach resort
is Alderman Island, one of several island wildlife
sanctuaries around the Coromandel Peninsula.

LEFT Tairua Harbour and Pauanui township
Each summer the bays, beaches, estuaries and
sheltered anchorages around the coast of the
Coromandel Peninsula are a magnet for thousands
of holidaying New Zealanders. Tairua, meaning 'the
place of two tides', is so named because there is a
high point nearby from which the tide of the Pacific
can be seen moving in the opposite direction from
the Firth of Thames tide, on the west of the peninsula.
Pauanui is a somewhat exclusive, purpose-built
holiday town.

ABOVE Hot Water Beach
A bonus for beachgoers here is the phenomenon of
hot water which seeps from submerged springs
through the sand two hours either side of low tide,
allowing them the luxury of scooping out their own,
personal (or family) 'spa'.

ABOVE **Tui**
One of New Zealand's best known native birds and
most prolific songsters, the tui is distinctive for the
tuft of white feathers under its neck. The honey-eating
tui is essentially a forest bird, but has thrived in
modified environments and is often seen (and heard)
feeding on nectar of plants in private gardens. Be
aware that the tui is also a skilful mimic!

RIGHT **Marokopa Falls between Kawhia
and Waitomo**
Forest-framed waterfalls are an endearing natural
feature throughout New Zealand. Many of these
waterfalls tumble through remnant areas of native
forest which have been declared scenic reserves, and
are thus protected. One third of all New Zealand is
legally protected as conservation land, in the form of
national and forest parks, and a multitude of reserves
and wildlife sanctuaries.

PREVIOUS PAGES Raglan farmland, Waikato
Early morning over lush Raglan farmland, near the east coast of the central North Island. During the 1800s much of New Zealand's native forest was cleared by settlers for farmland. For many years the sheep, dairy and beef industries were the country's leading export earners; more recently the tourism, forestry and wine industries have become important.

LEFT 'Lost World', Waitomo Caves
For many years taking a gentle walk was the only way to descend into the Waitomo Caves, followed by a short boat ride along an underground river to view glowworms. Now, in the adventurous New Zealand way, there are other options – abseiling, or rapelling, descents (some beneath underground waterfalls) by

'black water' rafting or tubing, swimming or even just jumping into subterranean pools. Descent into the Lost World cave is by a self-controlled, 100 metre, 15 minutes abseil, followed by a climb back to the surface through massive vaults.

ABOVE Catherwood's Cave, Waitomo Caves
The Waitomo area is honeycombed with limestone cave systems. Above the ground the landscape is one of rolling green hills and forest. Underground there is another landscape; of subterranean grottos and galleries draped with glistening limestone stalactites and stalagmites, many of them 'lit' by galaxies of glowworms. Waitomo's major 'show caves' have been captivating visitors for over a hundred years. Today, over 550,000 people visit each year.

LEFT Waihoro Lagoon, Pureora Forest Park
Kahikatea, or white pine, is the tallest and one of the oldest of the podocarp family. A special characteristic is that the tree likes 'wet feet', thus some of the most impressive stands of kahikatea are found in swampy lowland regions and wetlands, such as Waihoro Lagoon.

ABOVE Observation tower, Pureora Forest Park
Pureora contains some of New Zealand's finest podocarp forest. New Zealand naturalist, Sir Charles Fleming, referred to these giant rimu, miro, matai, totara and kahikatea trees as 'podocarp gothic' to compare them with the great cathedrals of Europe. In 1978, 'tree-sitting' conservationists stopped the felling of these trees and led to a government moratorium on clear felling, a landmark protest in the battle to end logging of native forest.
A short walk leads to the observation tower, where visitors can look into the upper branches of these giant trees. Chances are they will also see resident kaka and parakeets, native parrots.

ABOVE **Rotorua Museum of Art and History, Government Gardens**

Fiery geothermal and volcanic history and a strong association with Maori culture have been the bases of a long tourism tradition in and around Rotorua. The museum, housed in the Tudor-style building that was originally the Bath House and saw the birth of Rotorua's spa culture, exemplifies this heritage. The stories of Rotorua – of Te Arawa, the Maori people, the devastating 1886 Mt Tarawera eruption, geothermal activity and spa history are celebrated here. Outside, delightful walks lead through the gardens and lakeside geothermal spots.

RIGHT **Lake Rotoma**

The tranquillity of the twilight belies the fiery origins of Rotoma and the 16 other picturesque lakes dotted in forests around the region. Most are filled depressions and craters, blasted by volcanic eruption. Now, these lakes provide excellent habitat for many species of native freshwater fish and waterfowl. They are also stocked with introduced rainbow and brown trout – Rotorua is an internationally renowned fishery – and are popular holiday spots. As well as fishing, recreation pursuits include kayaking, water-skiing and sailing, and there are several lakeside camping areas and walkways.

LEFT Champagne Pool, Waiotapu Thermal Reserve, Rotorua

Waiotapu is one of the four geothermal fields around Rotorua open to visitors. As well as colourful and steaming features such as Champagne Pool, a large, bubbling alkaline spring, a major attraction here is the regularly performing Lady Knox Geyser. Other geyser fields are found at Hell's Gate and Whakarewarewa, where the star is Pohutu, one of the largest geysers in the world. Waimangu Valley features hot-water springs, steaming craters, sinter terraces and Lake Rotomahana, a legacy of the massive Mt Tarawera eruption in 1886.

ABOVE Geothermal mud pools, Rotorua

Rotorua sits on a volatile and spectacular region of volcanic and geothermal energy. Boiling mud pools, silica terraces, steaming vents (fumaroles), geysers and hot springs dot the landscape and a slightly pungent sulphuric odour pervades the air. For many years, tourists have come to marvel at these geothermal wonders, while the local people have learned to live with them, and developed them for use in cooking, bathing, medicines, dyes and rituals which are now an integral part of Maori tradition.

FOLLOWING PAGES Surfcasting, Rangitaiki River mouth, Bay of Plenty

The Rangitaiki River flows through forests from high on the central North Island plateau to meet the Pacific Ocean near Whakatane. Whatever the weather surfcasting fishermen, seeking a kahawai or any other fish that may take their bait, are a regular sight at river mouths and on beaches around the length of New Zealand's extensive coastline.

ABOVE **Fumaroles, White Island (Whakaari), Bay of Plenty**

The marine volcano of White Island is one of New Zealand's most active. Its sulphur-encrusted fumaroles, crater and vent are constantly steaming, hissing and roaring; an exhilarating experience for visitors to this fiery, moon-like terrain. Several tours, by sea or air, offer visits to the island, which is also an important place of study for international volcanologists.

The island is the first of the chain of volcanoes that traverses the centre of the North Island. All are part of the 'Pacific Rim of Fire', a vast belt of volcanic and earthquake activity encircling the Pacific.

RIGHT **Crater lake, White Island (Whakaari), Bay of Plenty**

The volcano's chemically coloured crater sits alongside its constantly steaming vent. The island's English name was given by Captain Cook, because it was covered in a cloud of white steam when he sailed past over 200 years ago. Nothing's changed.

LEFT Lottin Point (Wakatiri), East Cape
About as remote as one can be in New Zealand, the bays and rocky outcrops of Lottin Point are hidden down a side road. Line fishing from the rocks is good, though snorkelling among the myriad species of fish found in the deep blue sea here can be even more rewarding.

BELOW Makorori Beach
The coast north of Gisborne is lined with a succession of unspoiled beaches and bays, many of them the localities of small, predominantly Maori settlements. Surfing, swimming and gathering kai moana (sea food) are popular pastimes, particularly on beaches such as Makorori, 10 kilometres north of Gisborne.

LEFT **Tolaga Bay Wharf**
The 700 metre wharf is the longest in New Zealand. It was used by coastal shipping to service the district from 1929 until 1967 and is now a popular fishing spot. There is a small township at Tolaga Bay.

FOLLOWING PAGES **Poverty Bay flats, near Gisborne**
Orchards, maize paddocks and vineyards cover these rich alluvial flats; prime horticulture and cropping land. In the distance are the stunning white cliffs of Young Nick's Head, named after Captain Cook's look-out boy who first sighted land here in 1769.

LEFT Whirinaki River, Whirinaki Forest Park
The Whirinaki cuts a dramatic swathe through the
unyielding, ignimbrite walls of Te Whaiti Nui a Toi
Canyon. A high-quality path leads to a bridge across
the canyon, a fine viewpoint for this spectacle, just
15 minutes' walk from the car park. From the bridge
a tramping track continues alongside the Whirinaki,
which flows at a less pressured pace when not
hemmed between canyon walls, through the lofty
podocarp forest of Whirinaki Forest Park.

ABOVE Forest floor, Whirinaki Forest Park
A tangled profusion of understorey ferns and plants
covers the forest floor of Whirinaki, dwarfed by the
podocarp giants for which the park is known. Majestic
forests, filled with the lofty podocarps miro, rimu,
totara, matai and kahikatea, have risen from pumice
and ash thrown across the region by the massive
Taupo eruption of c. 186 AD.

LEFT **Korokoro Falls, Urewera National Park**
Urewera is one of New Zealand's largest national parks. Its remote mountain ranges are covered with dense podocarp and beech forest, part of the largest remaining tracts of forest in the North Island. Forest-framed waterfalls are a scenic feature. The Korokoro Falls can be reached via a short side track off the Lake Waikaremoana Track.

ABOVE **Trout fishing, Lake Waikaremoana, Urewera National Park**
Lake Waikaremoana is a gem in the heart of Te Urewera, a popular focus for recreation and, like everywhere else in the park, steeped in Maori tradition. One of New Zealand's premier walks, the Lake Waikaremoana Track, circles two-thirds of the lake. On the water, fishing and kayaking are popular. Although the protection of native species is paramount in national parks, introduced brown and rainbow trout live in the lake.

PREVIOUS PAGES **Te Mata Peak**
Sunrise lights the limestone buttresses of Te Mata
Peak. Walking tracks and a road lead to the more
gently sloping side of the peak (out of view); while
these eastern bluffs are an obvious and popular
launching spot for paragliders. On the right, the
Tukituki River nears the end of its seaward journey
from the inland ranges, one of several major waterways that deposit rich alluvium from the mountains
as they cross the Hawke's Bay plains. The fertile soils
and dry, sunny climate here produce prime conditions
for horticulture and vineyards.

LEFT AND BELOW **Cape Kidnappers**
Steep cliffs and sea-sprayed rock stacks at Cape
Kidnappers provide home to the world's largest mainland concentration of gannet colonies. Nearly 7000
pairs of gannets nest in several exposed, windswept
colonies at the cape, such as the Saddle colony (on
top of the cliffs at left) and Summit colony (below).
For bird-watching enthusiasts, these colonies are also
among the most accessible. Daily tours go to the
cape, and people can also walk there by following
the beach, an eight kilometre walk that's subject to
tide times.

LEFT TOP **Spirit of Napier statue, Marine Parade**
On February 3, 1931, a massive earthquake struck
Napier. The quake and ensuing fires devastated the
town centre and that of other, neighbouring towns. In
just two and a half minutes the quake caused massive
destruction. Some 4000 hectares of seabed was forced
upwards and 256 people died.
In the 1960s, to symbolise the rebirth of Napier, Frank
Szirmay sculpted the Spirit of Napier statue and
fountain. It stands among the gardens and walkways
of Napier's delightful Marine Parade.

LEFT BOTTOM **National Tobacco Company Ltd**
Following the destruction of the 1931 earthquake 'art deco' Napier rose from the ashes. New buildings followed the art deco style of the day, and the people of Napier have since taken such care to preserve the authenticity of the architecture that the city is now considered to have the most complete collection of art deco buildings in the world. The National Tobacco Company building, in Ahuriri, is one fine example. Guided tours of Napier's art deco buildings are run daily.

ABOVE **Tangoio Beach**
Hawke's Bay is blessed with fine beaches and sunny climate. Many beaches, such as Waipatiki, Ocean Beach and Waimarama, have long, glorious expanses of golden sands, gentle surf, are generally safe for swimming and are popular weekend and holiday spots. Beaches closer to the city, such as Tangoio, are of different character, still swimmable but more popular with surfcasters and beachcombers.

LEFT Lake Taupo
Tranquillity on New Zealand's largest lake, with the mountains Ruapehu (left) and Ngauruhoe standing guard in the distance. The calm belies the explosive history of this region, for the lake is in fact a massive volcano which exploded about 1800 years ago in one of the world's largest eruptions. Burning ash and rocks flung from the volcano flattened surrounding forests, and darkened skies from the eruption were recorded by early Chinese civilisations. At peace now, the lake is a popular fishing and holiday destination.

BELOW Kayaking, Waikato River
The Waikato is New Zealand's longest river and the outlet for Lake Taupo. Mountain water from the Tongariro volcanoes and central North Island mountains flows into Taupo, then pours into the rocky confines of the Waikato to start its 425 kilometre journey to the west coast, just south of Auckland. These kayakers can paddle only sections of the river. Soon after leaving Taupo the Waikato drops in foaming spectacle over Huka Falls, then passes through several hydro dams along its seaward journey.

PREVIOUS PAGES Mt Tongariro
Lunar-like terrain on Tongariro presents a stark
spectacle from the summit of Mt Ngauruhoe, which
is in fact a vent of the massive volcanic massif of
Tongariro. Craters, vents, lava flows and geothermal
springs on the mountain are all legacy of its volatile
history. On the lower slopes, forests have covered
scars of past volcanic anger but the landscape high on
the mountain is one of stark contrasts; the moon-like
terrain of Central Crater (foreground), contrasts with
Red Crater (middle) and Blue Lake, an old, filled
explosion crater.

LEFT Mt Ruapehu and The Grand Chateau
The mountains of Tongariro National Park lie at the
southern end of the 'Pacific Rim of Fire' volcanic zone.
Mt Ruapehu (2797m) is the highest of the three volcanic peaks and the most recently active. Nevertheless
the park is an extremely popular recreation destination, for winter skiing and climbing and short walks or
tramping in summer. At Whakapapa Village, The
Grand Chateau (foreground) has hosted guests in fine
style since 1929. There is also a campground, motels,
cafés and an excellent park visitor centre in the
village. Tongariro National Park is a World Heritage
Area, the first in the world to be granted dual status
for its natural and cultural values. The mountains are
of great spiritual significance to the local Maori
people.

RIGHT **Jersey heifers, Manawatu**
Dairy products are one of New Zealand's leading export industries. Major dairy farming areas are Waikato, Manawatu (where these heifers have been spotted grazing among the buttercups) and, increasingly in recent years, Southland.

FAR RIGHT **Farm barn, Ohakune**
Grassy paddocks, cleared of their original forest cover for farming, contrast sharply with dense forest over the fence, which marks the boundary of Tongariro National Park.

BELOW **Ohakune farmland and Mt Ruapehu**
Mt Ruapehu slumbers peacefully in the sun. However in successive eruptions in 1995 and 1996, the mountain showered these farms with clouds of volcanic ash.

LEFT Tama Lakes and Mt Ruapehu, Tongariro National Park
Walking tracks in Tongariro National Park explore a range of landscapes; from mature forests to subalpine shrublands to rocky scree. Volcanic landforms, water-falls over old lava flows and lakes that are filled explo-sion craters, such as Tama Lakes, are special features. One of New Zealand's premier walks, the Tongariro Circuit passes near these lakes as it crosses the high plateau between Mts Ruapehu and Ngauruhoe.

ABOVE Rangitikei River, near Mangaweka
Like many New Zealand rivers, the Rangitikei has cut its way through young and soft sedimentary siltstone rock, also known as papa. The Rangitikei begins its journey in the tussock-covered hills of Kaimanawa Forest Park, then cuts its way through fertile farmland to reach the sea near Bulls. The river is popular for fishing, canoeing and rafting.

LEFT **Farmland near Raetihi**
Raetihi is a small service town nestled between Mt Ruapehu and the provincial centre of Wanganui. It is one of the main access points to Whanganui National Park. Much of the original forest in this district has been milled, though remnant pockets of tawa, kamahi, black maire and some podocarps remain and are now protected in reserves. In many places scattered totara trees dot the farmland.

BELOW **Waterfall, Whanganui National Park**
The Whanganui is the longest continually navigable river in New Zealand. It passes through Whanganui National Park, a vast, rugged hinterland of lowland forest and in early times the river's gentle gradient formed a natural transport route for the Maori people who lived along its banks. Today, the Whanganui's scenic wilderness attracts thousands of canoeists. Waterfalls tumbling from side streams into the main river are a regular sight.

LEFT White Cliffs and Mt Taranaki, Tongaporutu, North Taranaki
The main highway through North Taranaki follows this dramatic coastline before heading inland to climb over the forest-covered Mt Messenger. At Tongaporutu, a side road leads to the White Cliffs Walkway, an exhilarating walk through the White Cliffs Conservation Area along these limestone cliffs, overlooking the Tasman Sea. Ever present, wherever one may be in the region, is the looming form of Mt Taranaki.

ABOVE North Island Brown Kiwi, inland Taranaki
The forested wilderness of inland Taranaki is home to one of the country's biggest populations of kiwi. The sturdy, flightless kiwi is unique in many ways and has become the national emblem; an icon representing the New Zealand 'spirit'. Kiwi are the smallest living members of the ratite family, which includes ostriches, emu and New Zealand's extinct moa. Loss of natural habitat and introduced predator animals have seriously reduced kiwi numbers, and a major conservation effort is underway to protect the six species that live throughout New Zealand.

FOLLOWING PAGES Mt Taranaki, Egmont National Park
The volcano Taranaki (2518m), first named by the Maori people then charted as Egmont in 1770 by Captain Cook, is the central focus of Egmont National Park. Other older and smaller, eroded volcanic mountains, such as Pouakai, and Potuha on the Kaitoke Range, lie to the north of Taranaki, still within the national park. Stunning mountain landscapes, such as this tussock-framed tarn on the Pouakai Range, are features of walking tracks in the park.

LEFT Powell Hut, Tararua Forest Park
Huts are a traditional legacy of New Zealand's back country. These small, basic huts are dotted throughout national and forest parks as shared, overnight accommodation for trampers, hunters and climbers. A minimal fee is payable to the Department of Conservation for their use; bookings are necessary for those on more popular walks, others are available on a first-come first-served basis. Powell Hut sits above bushline on the eastern Tararua Ranges.

BELOW Wellington viewed from Mt Alpha, Tararua Forest Park
Some of New Zealand's finest tramping country is found remarkably close to cities. The Tararua Ranges have for many years drawn wilderness-seeking city dwellers and the Tararua Tramping Club was the first of many such clubs to be formed in the country. In the southern ranges Mt Alpha (1361m) provides a fine viewing point of Wellington and Hutt Valley cities. Tapuae o Uenuku, of the Kaikoura Ranges, towers in the distance.

BELOW Lavender Farm, Te Horo, Horowhenua
The fertile Horowhenua plains, north of Wellington, are a major source of produce for Wellington city. Orchards, market gardens, dairy farms and herb fields are prolific. The lavender from this farm is harvested by hand then distilled with rainwater to produce essential oil, renowned for its therapeutic qualities.

BOTTOM Kapiti Island
Kapiti is one of New Zealand's largest and most significant island sanctuaries; a safe haven for many endangered wildlife species. Conservation staff have rid the island of all introduced pests, such as cats, rats and possums, which threaten New Zealand native birds and invertebrates. This view of the island's steep, western cliffs shows the magnitude of such work. The island is open to public visitation, by permit only.

PREVIOUS PAGES **Castlepoint, Wairarapa**
The last sun of the day adds to the show of
Castlepoint (Rangiwhakaoma), one of the most spectacular spots on the Wairarapa coast. The sheltered
lagoon, fossil-rich limestone reef, sand dunes and
Castle Rock itself are all part of Castle Point Scenic
Reserve. There are several walking tracks in the
vicinity, and surf casting is popular here. Castlepoint is
just over one hour's drive from the city of Masterton.

ABOVE **Wellington city and harbour, from Mt Kaukau**
Another day of commerce ends in the capital city,
and the night time cafés, clubs and restaurants will
be starting to hum. Nestled between hills and the
harbour (Te Whanganui a Tara: Great Harbour of Tara,
the first Maori settler), Wellington is rated among
the most picturesque cities in the world. Compact,
cosmopolitan and cultural, encircled by open,
windswept hills and with beaches and rocky coastline
only minutes from downtown, Wellington is a
beguiling city to live in or visit.

RIGHT **Parliament Buildings, Wellington**
Since 1865, Wellington has been New Zealand's capi-
tal city. Like successive governments and their poli-
cies, the architectural styles of Parliament's buildings
differ significantly. The Edwardian, neo-classical
Parliament House, featuring Coromandel granite and
Takaka marble, was completed in 1921. Alongside is
the Executive Wing, built in 1970 and nicknamed 'The
Beehive', for obvious reasons. Some of New Zealand's
other outstanding heritage buildings; the
Parliamentary Library, Wellington Cathedral,
Government Buildings and old St Paul's Cathedral, are
located within a block of Parliament.

LEFT **South coast**
Sandy beaches, rocky bays, surfing breaks and jagged
reefs where surf meets land in angry spectacle – a
drive around Wellington's southern coast will discover
all of these and none more than 10 minutes' drive
from the central city. After a southerly storm has
'washed' the city the air is typically crystalline and to
the south, across Cook Strait, Tapuae o Uenuku, the
highest mountain of the Kaikoura Range, can seem
close enough to touch.

BELOW **Cape Palliser lighthouse and bay**
Dusk at the southernmost tip of the North Island, and
as the South Pacific Ocean surges into Palliser Bay,
the Cape Palliser lighthouse signals its constant warning to coastal shipping. This is a bleak yet beautiful
piece of coastline to visit; the south coast road wends
its narrow way beneath steep coastal bluffs on one
side and surging surf and rocky outcrops on the other.
Along the way are the quaint fishing settlements of Te
Kopi and Ngawi, walking detours into Haurangi Forest
Park and the stunning Pinnacle limestone formations,
surfcasting and surfing beaches, shellfish spots, the
largest seal breeding colony in the North Island and,
finally, the lighthouse – only 250 steps to climb!

SOUTH ISLAND

Think South Island and one thinks big; in terms of mountains, glaciers, forests and snow-fed lakes and rivers. The mighty Southern Alps, crowned by New Zealand's highest mountain, Aoraki/Mt Cook, extend nearly the length of the island to form its main divide, a great jumble of mountains and glaciers.

On a different scale, something else that's special in the south is the wildlife – penguins, seals, marine mammals, and more. In many cases rare and endangered species live remarkably close to urban areas. Sperm whales feed closer to shore near Kaikoura than anywhere in the world, the only mainland colony of ocean-wandering royal albatross is beside Dunedin city and rare Hector's dolphins cavort in bays just minutes' drive from Christchurch, the South Island's biggest urban area.

Most cities and towns are located on the island's eastern side, where they support large scale farming, horticulture and viticulture enterprises. Tourism is also a major industry; key visitor attractions are natural heritage tours, outdoor adventure and tramping in the nine national parks and other parks, reserves and sanctuaries.

PREVIOUS PAGES **Kaikoura coastline**
Sunset over the Kaikoura coast, just north of the
whale-watching town; the Seaward Kaikoura
mountains stand behind.

ABOVE **Farewell Spit Nature Reserve**
Appropriately named Onetahua (heap of sand) by the
Maori people, Farewell Spit stretches 30 windswept
kilometres away from the northern tip of the South
Island. The spit provides an outstanding habitat for

migratory wading birds and is an internationally
recognised bird sanctuary. Farewell Spit tours
operate daily.

RIGHT **Archway Islands, Wharariki Beach,
Puponga Farm Park**
These spectacular rock stacks support breeding
colonies of fur seals, little blue penguins, terns and
shearwaters.

LEFT **Beech forest and tarn, Abel Tasman National Park**

Abel Tasman National Park is best known for its stunning coastline. Higher inland regions of the park are covered with dense, damp, mossy beech forest. Nothofagus (southern beech) covers over half the area of New Zealand's native forests.

ABOVE **Lake Sylvester, Cobb Valley tops, Kahurangi National Park**

The 'greenstone' coloured water of Lake Sylvester, 1325 metres high in the mountains, espouses the clarity and purity of New Zealand's alpine environment – and will surely have provided a welcome bathe for many a hot tramper! Sylvester is one of several lakes that nestle on the tussock tops above Cobb Valley in Kahurangi, New Zealand's second largest national park.

LEFT TOP **Bark Bay**
Where bush meets bay – the Abel Tasman coastline is
blessed with beautiful, bush-lined beaches, bays and
inlets. Accordingly it's an intensely popular visitor
destination. Sea kayakers paddle and yachties sail
along the coast by day, and venture into sheltered
anchorages or campsites by night. Each year
thousands of people walk the Abel Tasman Coastal
Track, staying in huts and campsites along the way.

LEFT BOTTOM **Bark Bay estuary**
With so many diverse habitats, marine life thrives
along the coast of the park. Dolphins and seals, sea
birds and wading birds, ocean fish and estuarine fish,
and underwater plant and animal communities equal
to or better than those anywhere in New Zealand
thrive in and around the clean ocean water, rocky
reefs, estuaries and bays. The forests provide a home
for many species of native forest birds, and native
fresh-water fish live in park streams, free from the
threat of introduced trout that prey on native fish.

ABOVE **Kotuku, white heron**
Wetlands and estuaries around New Zealand host
hundreds of thousands of wading birds, many of them
seasonal visitors who fly incredible migratory routes
from the Northern Hemisphere. Other birds, such as
the kotuku, migrate to winter feeding grounds within
New Zealand. The kotuku is the rarest of New
Zealand's four heron species. Self-introduced from
Australia (birds have blown across the Tasman Sea),
it breeds at Okarito Lagoon in south Westland.

FOLLOWING PAGES **Totaranui**
Golden beach after golden beach line the coast of
Abel Tasman National Park. Totaranui is one of the
larger visitor choices and a main park access point.
These occupants are fortunate to be sharing Totaranui
with so few. In summer especially, this coastline is
extremely popular. To help protect the natural
environs and avoid over-crowding, bookings are
required to stay in huts along the Abel Tasman
Coastal Walk, which as its name suggests follows
the coastline of the park.

LEFT **Pelorus Sound from Mt Stokes**
Hues of blues as the beech-framed hills recede.
Mt Stokes (1203m) is the highest point of the
Marlborough Sounds.

ABOVE TOP **Maud Island**
Many islands in the sounds are wildlife sanctuaries;
the last refuges for some species that no longer
survive on the mainland because of introduced pred-
ators, such cats and rats. Several island sanctuaries
are open to the public. Others, such as Maud Island,
are restricted to protect their fragile environments.

ABOVE **Takahe adult and chick, Maud Island**
One of the rarest species surviving on Maud Island
is the flightless takahe. For 50 years the bird was
thought to be extinct, until it was rediscovered in
Fiordland. Takahe have since been raised on island
sanctuaries, such as Maud.

ABOVE Picton, Marlborough Sounds
The immaculately groomed Picton foreshore provides
a fine welcome for arrivals from the North Island.
Picton is the southern port for the Interislander ferry
services which cross Cook Strait from Wellington.
There is a strong tourism focus in the town. Picton is
close to the Marlborough wine-growing region, and
the main stepping-off point for Queen Charlotte
Sound. Popular activities in the Sound include mountain biking and walking the Queen Charlotte Walkway,
ecotourism cruises, sea kayaking, sailing and fishing.

RIGHT Wairau Lagoons
These lagoons rate among the country's most significant estuarine wetlands. Over 70 species of birds have
been recorded here, among them terns, shags, oyster-
catchers, godwits and royal spoonbills. The lagoons
are also archaeologically important. The discovery
here of moa bones, belonging to large, flightless ratite
birds which became extinct in the 1600s, along with
signs of human occupation, provided important
scientific knowledge of the very first Maori settlers in
this country, known to some as the 'moa-hunters'. The
lagoons are six kilometres from Blenheim. A walking
track leads through the wetlands and marshes.

ABOVE Wairau Valley, Marlborough
A dry, sunny climate and unique soil conditions make
the Wairau a most productive valley for agriculture,
and horticulture, in particular grape growing. In the
past 20 years the Marlborough wine industry has
burgeoned. There are now more than 50 wineries in
the region and Marlborough sauvignon blancs,
chardonnays, pinot noirs and méthode champenoise
are regular winners of national and international
awards.

RIGHT Cape Campbell, Marlborough
Lighthouses have been guiding coastal shipping
around the 7000 kilometres of New Zealand coastline
since 1859. Up until the 1980s many of these were
manned, and a number of lighthouse keepers and
their families lived on remote outposts and islands.
Now all lights are automatic. Cape Campbell guards
the entrance to Clifford Bay, southeast of Blenheim.
In recent years a number of whale strandings have
occurred around the cape.

LEFT TOP **Awatere River Valley and Mt Tapuae o Uenuku, Marlborough**
The growing wine industry of Marlborough has spread southwards to Awatere Valley, where hundreds of hectares have been planted in grapes in recent years. The Awatere flats are built from river gravels and fine dust known as loess, a product of a past glacial era and blown down-valley by the wind. The Awatere Valley road provides good views of the Inland Kaikoura mountains, and is the main access for climbing their highest peak, Tapuae o Uenuku.

LEFT BOTTOM AND BELOW **Acheron Accommodation House, Molesworth Station, Marlborough**
Historic Molesworth is New Zealand's biggest farm, supports the largest herd of cattle and is one of the country's major farming and conservation achievements. Farm management is undertaken in conjunction with the Department of Conservation, which oversees protection of the special natural qualities of the 180,000 hectare, high-country run. The 50 kilometre road through Molesworth is open to the public each summer and is particularly popular with mountain bikers. The historic Acheron Accommodation House (built in 1863) is one of two cobb-constructed cottages available for overnight stays.

ABOVE **Kerr Bay, Lake Rotoiti**
Nelson Lakes is named for its two lakes, Rotoiti and
Rotoroa (meaning 'small' lake and 'long' lake), which
nestle in picturesque grandeur between steep, forest-
covered mountains. As the jetty suggests, boating is
a popular recreation on Rotoiti.

RIGHT **Roberts Ridge**
Daybreak on the heights of Roberts Ridge, one of the
most accessible and popular tramping routes in the
park (when the weather is suitable on this exposed,
open ridge). Thick cloud on the left hides Lake Rotoiti,
far below.

FOLLOWING PAGES **Kaikoura Ranges, Marlborough**
The two mountain ranges of Kaikoura, the inland and
seaward ranges, are divided by the Clarence River.
The Awatere River, covered in cloud on the right,
drains the western flanks of the inland range. The
ranges are isolated from the main alpine fault that
built the mighty Southern Alps, they are geologically
young and undergoing the fastest uplift of any New
Zealand mountains. At 2885m Mt Tapuae o Uenuku
is the highest point. Kaikoura peninsula can be seen
in the distant left.

LEFT AND ABOVE **Kaikoura**

There are few places with a diversity of marine life, so easy to see, in such a stunning mountain-meets-sea setting, as Kaikoura. Sperm whales (top) come closer to shore here than anywhere in the world, feeding on deep-water fish and giant squid that live in deep undersea canyons just off shore. Migratory humpback and pilot whales and orcas call past. Hector's, common and dusky dolphins (above) live in local waters and fur seal colonies inhabit the coastline (right beside the main road). Ecotourism has become a major focus in Kaikoura and a host of whale, dolphin, seal and sea bird-watching cruises attract thousands of international visitors each year.

ABOVE **Spenser Mountains, Lewis Pass**
A mountain lake reflecting beech forest with a back-
drop of snow-covered mountains; it's a classic New
Zealand image. The setting is near Lewis Pass, close
to the start of the St James Walkway, a five-day walk
bordering the Lewis Pass National Reserve and high-
country farmland in north Canterbury. Lewis Pass is
one of the few road passes that cross the South
Island's Southern Alps.

RIGHT **Devil's Punchbowl Falls from Avalanche Peak
Track, Arthur's Pass National Park**
Arthur's Pass is one of the easiest places to access the
mountain environment of the Southern Alps, for the
spectacular highway through the park crosses the
highest of the few passes over the main divide. Huge,
ice-gouged hanging valleys, massive slopes filled with
avalanching scree, waterfalls, forests and alpine
meadows – all these are park characteristics which
can be seen from the road. There are also many short
walks, to features such as the Devil's Punchbowl Falls,
and tramping tracks which explore the park's long
valleys and mountain ridges and peaks.

LEFT Punting on the Avon River, Christchurch
Christchurch is regarded as the most English of New Zealand's cities, a legacy emanating from the first English settlers who arrived here in 1850. Heritage buildings in the city, the Gothic Cathedral, Arts Centre and Canterbury Museum, along with parks and gardens and the tree-lined Avon River that wends its way through the heart of the city, enhance the 'English-ness' of the South Island's largest urban centre. Continuing the English theme, punting the Avon is a traditional 'Christchurch' thing to do.

ABOVE Christchurch Cathedral, Christchurch
The spire of this magnificent English Gothic cathedral once dominated the city skyline. Today, though overlooked by office towers and hotels, it remains the symbolic centre of Christchurch. The cathedral's first foundation stone was laid in 1864, however the ambitious project for a then fledgling town endured protracted delays. The main body, or nave, was opened in 1881 and the rituals of worship, choral music and bell ringing that began then continue today. The cathedral was finally completed in 1904, a visitor centre and café was added in 1994. Over 500,000 people visit each year, and also enjoy the surrounding ambience of the very English Cathedral Square.

LEFT TOP Hector's dolphins, Akaroa Harbour
Although one of the world's rarest and smallest
dolphins, Hector's dolphins can nevertheless be easy
to find – if looking in the right place! Most live around
Banks Peninsula and the South Island west coast, and
they generally live close to shore. To protect these
rare dolphins, set-net fishing has been banned and
a marine mammal sanctuary established around
Banks Peninsula.

LEFT BOTTOM **Little blue penguin**
New Zealand's smallest and most widespread penguin
species; little blues live around the coastline of New
Zealand, in many cases close to urban areas. They are
known to nest beneath seaside homes, a not always
popular occurrence considering the noise a nesting
pair will generate during their breeding season. This
one is of the white-flippered variety, which lives
around the Banks Peninsula coastline.

ABOVE **Akaroa**
Settled in 1840 by French colonists, modern Akaroa
has made a point of retaining its special, 'French
village' character. Cafés, craft galleries and wine bars,
many housed in colonial-style buildings, add to the
ambience of the sheltered, seaside settlement.
Another major focus of Akaroa is the choice of wildlife
cruises on Akaroa Harbour, to see penguins, seals, sea
birds and the rare Hector's dolphins living in their
natural environments.

ABOVE **Mount Cook lily (Ranunculus lyalli)**
This giant mountain buttercup, often misnomered
the Mount Cook lily, is an iconic symbol of
Aoraki/Mt Cook National Park. It flowers in summer
(November to January) and also grows in other alpine
regions of the Southern Alps. Buttercups, gentians,
mountain daisies, hebe species and a host of other
alpine flowers brighten walking paths in many easily
accessible spots of Aoraki/Mt Cook and Arthur's Pass
national parks.

RIGHT **Aoraki/Mt Cook**
The summit of New Zealand's highest mountain,
Aoraki/Mt Cook (3754m), is sharply reflected in one of
the Sealy Tarns, small, alpine lakes which nestle on a
tussock terrace, two hours' climb from the valley floor.

FOLLOWING PAGES **Mt Tasman and the Southern
Alps/Ka Tiritiri o te Moana**
In Maori mythology the South Island landmass is the
upturned canoe of the revered ancestor, Aoraki. When
the canoe capsized, Aoraki and his crew climbed to
the high side of the wreck and became the great
southern mountains.

LEFT Oparara River, Karamea, Kahurangi National Park
Beech trees overhang the tannin-stained Oparara River, on the western side of Kahurangi National Park. In the Oparara valley, arches and caves, the result of subterranean streams sculpting the soft limestone rock, are a distinctive feature.

ABOVE Koura Beach, Heaphy Track, Kahurangi National Park
The Heaphy Track is one of New Zealand's premier tramping tracks. Its great charm is its landscape diversity; the four-to six-day walk traverses a beech-forested valley, open tussocklands, dense rainforest and remote, rocky coastline.

BELOW Fox River, Paparoa National Park
Nature's art; limestone sculptures and the carving work of water are the special features of Paparoa National Park. Rivers in the park have sculpted its soft limestone base into deep chasms and canyons. The Fox River, and especially the Fox River Cave – a popular visitor attraction – showcase some of the park's finest limestone formations.

LEFT Pancake Rocks, Paparoa National Park
Stormy seas and sky; one of New Zealand's most
popular short walks leads to this stunning sight at
Punakaiki, where westerly sea swells surge against
these extraordinary layered limestone stacks and
erupt in geyser-like explosions from underwater
chasms. The path to these rocks and blowholes is
of very high standard, suitable for wheelchairs.

ABOVE Lake Brunner and Hohonu Range, Westland
Majestic kahikatea forests thrive in the moist
conditions surrounding wetlands and lakes such as
Brunner, the largest lake in Westland. Like much of
the South Island landscape, Lake Brunner has been
shaped by the powerful forces of ice. The lake fills an
ancient glacial depression, dammed by a moraine. It
is named after an intrepid New Zealand explorer,
Thomas Brunner.

ABOVE **Okarito Lagoon, Westland**
Sanctuary for the birds; Okarito Lagoon is the largest
remaining natural estuary in New Zealand, and a bird-
watcher's paradise. Sheltered from westerly ocean
swells by bouldery beaches, the lagoon supports
thousands of native and migratory birds and is the
main feeding ground of royal spoonbills and white
herons (kotuku). The kotuku breed in nearby kahikatea
trees, alongside the Waitangiroto River which drains
into the lagoon.

RIGHT **Franz Josef/Ka Roimata o Hine Hukatere
Glacier, Westland/Tai Poutini National Park**
There are few places in the world where glaciers exist
at such temperate latitudes, and are so accessible to
tourists, as in Westland/Tai Poutini National Park.
Throughout the park there are over 60 glaciers; great
rivers of ice grinding their way down the park's
valleys, eventually melting as they reach warmer
temperatures, only a few miles from the sea. These
glaciers have shaped the landscape of the park.

ABOVE Rainforest
In South Westland dense rainforests, filled with lofty
rimu and kahikatea trees and crowded with lower-
growing trees and ferns and shrubs, thrive in the mild
temperatures and heavy rainfall. These forests are
part of Te Wahi Pounamu World Heritage Area, a massive region that encompasses the mountains, glaciers,
valleys and forests of Aoraki/Mt Cook, Westland/Tai
Poutini, Mt Aspiring and Fiordland national parks.

RIGHT Haast River tributary
Creeks tumble through mossy banks in the rainforest
of Westland to meet bigger rivers such as the Haast,
which in its lower reaches meanders over broad, open
flats alongside the Haast Pass highway, the southern-
most pass over the main divide.

**FOLLOWING PAGES Lake Leeb and Mt Aspiring/Tititea,
Mt Aspiring National Park**
The classic, alpine horn-shape Mt Aspiring (3027m)
(left) is called Tititea, or glistening peak, by the Maori
people. Aspiring is flanked by snowfields, mountain
ranges and great, glacier-gouged valleys. Lake Leeb
nestles among tussock and snow, high on the
Thomson Range in the remote, south-western
corner of the park.

PREVIOUS PAGES Moeraki Boulders
The sun sets over the Moeraki boulders, described by local Maori as petrified food baskets washed ashore from a wrecked ancestral canoe. Inevitably there is also a scientific explanation for these geological curiosities; they are deemed to be 60 million year-old 'concretions' formed by the reactions of lime minerals in seabed sediments. The boulders, each weighing several tonnes, have fallen to the beach from eroding sea cliffs.

ABOVE Otago Harbour and Macandrew Bay
A 20-minute drive from the centre of Dunedin City leads to rural Otago Peninsula and Macandrew Bay (named after a city founder). The peninsula extends along the far side of the harbour (which was formed by a massive, ancient volcano) from the city. Its coastline is home to some of the world's rarest wildlife species; yellow-eyed penguins, New Zealand sea lions and northern royal albatross. Several wildlife watching tours are available from Dunedin.

LEFT Royal Albatross (toroa), Otago Peninsula
Nowhere in the world does the Northern Royal
Albatross nest so close to human settlement as on
Taiaroa Head, Otago Peninsula. The ocean-crossing
albatross, which rank among the world's largest
seabirds, usually nest in the remote, hostile environment of the Subantarctic Islands. The Otago Peninsula
colony first became established in the early 1900s,
and has subsequently provided a unique opportunity
for ornithologists, scientists and other visitors to
observe these majestic birds at close hand.

**BELOW Yellow-eyed Penguin (hoiho), Otago
Peninsula**
One of the world's rarest and smallest species of
penguin, the hoiho live around the coastline of Otago
Peninsula. Hoiho numbers became threatened when
their coastal shrub nesting habitat was disturbed by
farming development, however a public campaign to
save the species, together with conservation and
revegetation measures by Peninsula farmers, have
resulted in a significant resurgence of numbers.

BELOW Hawkdun Range
When books are published about Central Otago they tend not to be text-filled chronicles of regional history and geography but rather more artistic tomes; their pages filled with poetry and paintings. Such is the physical nature of 'Central'; stark landscape, clear air, frostily cold in winter and dry, searing heat in summer, it inspires such artistry.

RIGHT Blue Lake, St Bathans
For the heat of a Central Otago summer there's a simple answer; go jump in the lake. Blue Lake was formed by gold-sluicing operations in the 1860s, when St Bathans was a busy gold-mining settlement. Today the well-preserved goldworkings and stone and mud-brick buildings are part of the Otago Goldfields Park.

FOLLOWING PAGES Cribs at Poolburn Reservoir
Cribs are South Island-speak for a weekend or holiday home. These are often located by a beach, or lake, and are generally fairly basic, suitable for full concentration on whatever relaxing pursuit may be desired in the location, be it fishing, walking, boating, or simply reading a book. In the North Island cribs are called baches. Whatever their moniker the concept is a long-time New Zealand tradition.

LEFT **Cardrona Skifield, near Wanaka**
One of four ski resorts in the Wanaka/Queenstown region, Cardrona is purported to be 'wider, higher and drier' than neighbouring fields. International snowboard events are held here.

BELOW **West Matukituki Valley, Mt Aspiring National Park**
The West Matukituki, one of the many valley tramping routes in the park, is also an access route for climbing Mt Aspiring.

BOTTOM **Lake Harris, Routeburn Track**
A premier spot on one of New Zealand's premier walking tracks.

LEFT Remarkable Mountains, Lake Wakatipu and Queenstown
Queenstown, which began as a service town for gold-miners and runholders, has today become one of New Zealand's major tourist destinations. This view, from the Skyline Gondola which climbs Ben Nevis behind the town, clearly shows why the region is so popular. The local tourism industry has developed a multitude of visitor options for enjoying and experiencing the region's natural splendour.

ABOVE TSS *Earnslaw*, Lake Wakatipu
Affectionately known as the 'Lady of the Lake', TSS *Earnslaw* has been carrying goods to remote settlements and passengers on scenic cruises on mountain-lined Lake Wakatipu since 1912. The steamer is one of the last remaining coal-fired, passenger-carrying vessels operating in the Southern Hemisphere. She provides a tranquil option for enjoying the scenery, given that Queenstown is at times referred to as the 'adventure capital of the south'. Bungy jumping, jet-boating, white water rafting, parapenting, heliskiing and snowboarding are other local choices.

BELOW **Kea, mountain parrot, Fiordland National Park**

Visitors to South Island high-country regions are likely to witness the cheeky high jinks of the kea, one of New Zealand's native parrots, though humour can quickly turn to anger when such antics become damaging to expensive outdoor equipment. Kea are related to other New Zealand parrots the kaka, the bush parrot, and kakapo, the flightless and heaviest of all parrots and one of the world's most endangered birds.

RIGHT **MacKay Falls, Milford Track, Fiordland National Park**

Once defined as 'the finest walk in the world' the Milford Track has been a drawcard for international hikers for over a hundred years. The walk traverses two valleys and an alpine pass in the Fiordland mountains. Waterfalls crashing steeply down sheer mountainsides, or cascading over boulders in dense rainforest, are a feature of the walk. While the track's 580 metre-high Sutherland Falls may be more dramatic, the MacKay Falls are also memorable.

BELOW **Arthur Valley, Milford Track**
It's all downhill from here! Having climbed from the
Clinton Valley floor to Mackinnon Pass, the Milford
Track descends steeply into Arthur Valley, then traces
its rainforested way to the track's end, at Milford
Sound/Piopiotahi.

RIGHT **Mackinnon Memorial and Pass, Milford Track**
The highest point of the Milford Track, Mackinnon
Pass is a fine vantage point from which to survey the
majesty of Fiordland's mountains. Although officially
'discovered' by Quinton Mackinnon in 1888 it is likely
others had climbed the pass before. Mackinnon later
became a self-appointed guide for the first people
who walked the newly discovered route from Lake Te
Anau to Milford Sound/Piopiotahi.

FOLLOWING PAGES **Hollyford Valley from Conical Hill,
Routeburn Track**
One of New Zealand's most famous tracks is the
Routeburn, which traverses mountainous terrain of Mt
Aspiring and Fiordland National Parks, through a
delightful mix of rainforest, tussock grasslands, summer-flowering herbfields, mountain streams, waterfalls
and lakes, all hemmed by towering mountain peaks.
Conical Hill is a short though steep detour from the
track's highest point, Harris Saddle. Looking from here
into the Hollyford's headwaters, the Routeburn Track
can be seen above the forest on the left of the valley.

LEFT Milford Sound/Piopiotahi, Fiordland National Park

RIsing steeply from the sound, Mitre Peak (left), is probably the most photographed mountain in New Zealand. Frenetic scenic flight and tourist coach schedules bring thousands of sightseers to the sound each day, and the impact of tourism is carefully monitored by park managers to ensure the natural integrity of this majestic place is unaffected.

According to Maori, Milford/Piopiotahi was the last and most perfect of the great fiords carved by hand by legendary ancestor, Tu Te Rakiwhano. However, he decided his work was too perfect, so for balance introduced namu, the sandfly, which has antagonised visitors to Fiordland ever since.

ABOVE Stirling Falls, Milford Sound/Piopiotahi, Fiordland National Park

Nearly 150m high, yet these falls are dwarfed by the surrounding mountains. After heavy rain, hundreds of waterfalls that plunge down these sheer mountain sides create a classic and memorable Fiordland sight. The Stirling Falls cascade from an ice-gouged hanging valley, another classic feature of Fiordland, where much of the landscape has been shaped by great glaciers of past ice ages.

FOLLOWING PAGES Lake Erskine, looking toward Mt Tutoko, Fiordland National Park

'Mountains of water' is an apt description of Fiordland, a massive expanse of glaciated mountains, fiord-indented coastline, lakes, rivers and the largest tract of native forest in New Zealand. The park forms a major part of the Te Wahi Pounamu World Heritage Area. Mt Tutoko (2746m) is Fiordland's highest mountain.

LEFT Tautuku Beach, Catlins
The primeval Catlins, on the South Island's remote, southeastern coastline, where tall, podocarp forests grow to the edge of beaches and estuaries.

ABOVE Slope Point, Catlins
Sure it's sunny, but the wind-bent macrocarpa trees show what the weather's really like at this southern-most point of the South Island.

BELOW Fur seal pups, Catlins
Seals, whose numbers have recovered after near decimation by seal hunters in the 1800s, share the Catlins coastline with several endangered marine wildlife species; New Zealand sea lions, yellow-eyed penguins and Hector's dolphins.

FOLLOWING PAGES Nugget Point, Catlins
Shipping warning, scenic spectacle and wildlife haven, Nugget Point is home to sea lions, seals, penguins, shags and a host of seabirds.

ABOVE White capped (shy) mollymawk
Albatrosses and mollymawks, the great, ocean-wandering pelagics of the stormy South Pacific and Subantarctic seas, regularly 'come fishing' near the South Island east coast and Stewart Island. Mollymawk is the term used for smaller species of albatross. With the exception of royal albatross, which breed on the mainland at Tairoa Head, Otago, these birds breed in colonies on remote southern islands, mainly the remote Subantarctic group, over 200 kilometres southeast of New Zealand.

RIGHT Ernest Islands and Mason Bay
Mason Bay and the rocky Ernest Islands lie on the remote west of Stewart Island/Rakiura, away from the eastern settlement of Halfmoon Bay. North of Mason Bay is Whenua Hou (Codfish Island) Nature Reserve, refuge for the rare kakapo, ground parrot, and one of New Zealand's most important island sanctuaries.

RIGHT **Ernest Islands**
A storm approaches a stormy coastline. Set apart geographically on the subantarctic edge of New Zealand, Stewart Island/Rakiura has been left largely to nature's devices and is a treasure chest of un-modified ecosystems and habitats, a haven for rare plants and endangered wildlife. New Zealand's newest and fifth largest national park, Rakiura encompasses nearly all the land area of Stewart Island/Rakiura and many of its offshore islands.

FOLLOWING PAGE **Big Kuri Bay**
Of all the landscapes of Rakiura – sea-pounded cliffs, forests of lofty rimu, kahikatea and totara, wetlands, dunelands, shrublands and rocky mountain ranges – the forest-fringed golden beaches, so many of them remote and rarely visited, exemplify the primeval character of the island. Visitors do make their way to Stewart Island/Rakiura; they fly or boat across Foveaux Strait to explore its scenic and wildlife won-ders. Tramping, sea kayaking, hunting (for introduced deer) and wildlife watching are popular activities.